Pondering Tidbits of Truth

(Volume 4)

Compiled and Edited
by
Michael Seagriff

Pondering Tidbits of Truth

(Volume 4)

Copyright © 2017 by Michael Seagriff

All rights reserved. No part of this book may be used or reproduced by any means, graphic, electronic, or mechanical, including photocopying, recording, taping or by any information storage retrieval system without the written permission of the publisher except in the case of brief quotations embodied in critical articles and reviews.

ISBN - 13: 9780578198552
ISBN - 10: 057819855X

Printed in the United States of America

Michael Seagriff
Canastota, New York

Dedication

To all hungry souls seeking to learn,
live and share the Truth

Table of Contents

Introduction vii
Quotations
[1]   St. Augustine   1
[2]   St. Josemaria Escriva   1
[3]   Jean-Baptiste Henri Lacordaire, O.P.   1
[4]   Venerable Pope Pius XII   2
[5]   Catherine de Hueck Doherty, Servant of God   2
[6]   St. Augustine   2
[7]   Blessed Alvaro del Portillo   3
[8]   St. Theophilus of Antioch   3
[9]   Paul Thigpen, PhD.   3
[10] St. John Paul II   3
[11] St. Teresa of Calcutta   4
[12] St. Augustine   4
[13] Father Jose Orlandis   4
[14] Father Benedict Baur, O.S.B.   4
[15] St. Ambrose   5
[16] St. John Paul II   5
[17] St. John of the Cross   6
[18] St. Josemaria Escriva   6
[19] St. Francis de Sales   6
[20] Thomas Aquinas, O.P.   6
[21] St. John Paul II   7
[22] Venerable Fulton J. Sheen   7
[23] Father Eugene Boylan, O.C.R.   7
[24] St. John Chrysostom   8
[25] St. Francis de Sales   8
[26] Father Francis Wendell, O.P.   8
[27] St. John Paul II   9
[28] Father Francis Fernandez   9
[29] St. Catherine of Siena   9

[30]	St. Josemaria Escriva	9
[31]	St. Bede	10
[32]	Venerable Louis of Granada, O.P.	10
[33]	St. Augustine	10
[34]	St. John Paul II	11
[35]	Venerable Fulton J Sheen	11
[36]	Vatican Council II	11
[37]	Blessed Pope Paul VI	11
[38]	C.S. Lewis	12
[39]	Father Federico Suarez	12
[40]	St. Thomas Aquinas, O.P.	12
[41]	St. Josemaria Escriva	13
[42]	St. Alphonsus Liguori	13
[43]	St. Theophilus of Antioch	13
[44]	St. John Paul II	13
[45]	Marie Dominique Philippe, O.P.	14
[46]	Justice Antonin Scalia	14
[47]	St. Vincent of Lerins	15
[48]	St. John Paul II	15
[49]	St. Alphonsus Liguori	15
[50]	St. John Chrysostom	16
[51]	Blessed John Henry Newman	16
[52]	St. Thomas Aquinas, O.P.	16
[53]	St. Bernard of Clairvaux	16
[54]	St. John Paul II	16
[55]	St. Augustine	17
[56]	Father Federico Suarez	17
[57]	Father Francis Fernandez	17
[58]	St. Alphonsus Liguori	18
[59]	St. John Paul II	18
[60]	Francis Sheed	18
[61]	C. Lopez Pardo	19
[62]	Jean-Baptiste Chautard, O.C.S.O.	19

[63]	Reginald Garrigou-Lagrange, O.P.	20
[64]	St. Augustine	20
[65]	Caryll Houselander	20
[66]	Blessed John Paul VI	20
[67]	St. Mechtildis	21
[68]	St. Jerome	21
[69]	St. Francis de Sales	21
[70]	St. Josemaria Escriva	21
[71]	St. Leo the Great	22
[72]	St. Alphonsus Liguori	22
[73]	Madeleine Delbrel, Servant of God	22
[74]	Brother Lawrence of the Resurrection	22
[75]	St. Teresa of Avila	23
[76]	Juan Donoso Cortes	23
[77]	St. Augustine	23
[78]	Blessed Henry Suso, O.P.	24
[79]	St. Josemaria Escriva	24
[80]	Vatican II	24
[81]	St. John Paul II	25
[82]	Catherine de Hueck Doherty, Servant of God	25
[83]	Father Federico Suarez	25
[84]	St. Alphonsus Liguori	25
[85]	Father Francis Fernandez	26
[86]	Cardinal Pietro Parolin	26
[87]	Whittaker Chambers	26
[88]	St. Augustine	27
[89]	St. Bernard of Clairvaux	27
[90]	Pope Pius XI	27
[91]	Rev. M. Raymond, O.C.S.O.	28
[92]	Catherine de Hueck Doherty, Servant of God	28
[93]	Brother Lawrence of the Resurrection	29
[94]	Father Charles Armijon	29
[95]	St. Maximilian Kolbe	29

[96]	Father Jacques Phillipe	30
[97]	Rev. M. Raymond, O.C.S.O.	30
[98]	St. Pius X	30
[99]	St. Augustine	31
[100]	Blessed Alvaro del Portillo	31

Individuals Quoted   32
Suggested Reading   36
About the Author   39
Other Books by Author   40

Pondering Tidbits of Truth – Volume 4

"There is great turmoil at this time in the world and in the Church, and what is in dispute is the faith…What strikes me, when I look at the Catholic world, is that within Catholicism a sort of non-Catholic thought seems to predominate sometimes, and it may happen tomorrow that this non-Catholic thought will become the strongest within Catholicism. But it will never represent the mind of the Church. A tiny little flock has to continue in existence, however small it may be."

Blessed Pope Paul VI

Pondering Tidbits of Truth – Volume 4

Introduction

Are you among the countless souls who never seem to have enough time in the day to get through your "To Do" list?

Have you promised God that you would "fit Him" in that busy schedule of yours, but have been unsuccessful in doing so?

Have you recently discovered an insatiable hunger to learn or relearn essential truths of your Catholic Faith but don't know where or how to begin?

Are you hesitant to discuss or share your Faith with others because you are afraid you will not be able to do so effectively?

Maybe you are one of those persons who has been unable to get through the spiritual classics but would benefit from the work of someone who has spent time compiling excerpts from those treasures.

Do you fall in that group of people who have heretofore approached spiritual reading as being worse than going to a dentist?

Perhaps you have not yet seen the value in making time for spiritual reading in your daily life.

Let's be honest. Maybe you have just been too lazy to even attempt to do so. Haven't we all been there?

Whatever the reason, you have no excuses anymore to suffer spiritual malnutrition.

This volume of *Pondering Tidbits of Truths*, like its three predecessors, presents 100 potentially life-changing quotations for you to read and ponder, one morsel at a time, at your own pace and at a time of the day that you find most convenient – when your first begin the day, during your coffee or lunch break, while you in the waiting room of your doctor, or before settling in for the night.

Take the first step today. Read the first quotation, as many times as it takes before you hear something in it that speaks to your heart and soul.

You can do this! You should do this! You need to do this!

Then read another passage. Keep reading at least one each day. When you are done go back and ponder them again and again. You will likely find something new. You will also be amazed how God will use these words to make of you a new creation.

QUOTATIONS

[1]   St. Augustine

We cannot keep ourselves on the road to perfection and prevent ourselves from failing except by efforts to climb higher. As soon as we begin to stop, we regress, with the result that, if we do not wish to fall back, we have to run ahead always, without slowing down.

(From *Instructions for Novices* by Blessed Hyacinthe-Marie Cormier, O.P.)

[2]   St. Josemaria Escriva

It looks as if the whole world is coming down on top of you. Whichever way you turn you find no way out. This time, it is impossible to overcome the difficulties. But have you forgotten that God is your Father? All-powerful, infinitely wise, full of mercy. He would never send you anything that is evil. That thing that is worrying you, it's good for you, even though those earthbound eyes of yours may not be able to see it now. 'Omnia in bonum!' Lord, once again and always, may your most wise Will be done.

(From *The Way of the Cross*)

[3]   Jean-Baptiste Henri Lacordaire, O.P.

What is difficult is to carry the cross each day, the cross which is not blood-stained but which bruises the skin a little without making it bleed, and which is composed of restraint, tediousness and languor. If one could only mount Calvary once and for all, and give one's body once and for all to the executioners, what pleasure! But no, the torment is in detail; a little cut of the whip, a little slap in the face, a little humiliation.

(From *St. Dominic's Family* by Sister Mary Jean Dorcy, O.P.)

[4] Venerable Pope Pius XII

God lets Himself be seen by those who are able to see Him because they have the eyes of their soul open. Everyone has eyes, but the eyes of some are blinded as it were in darkness and they cannot see the light of the sun. But the light of the sun does not cease to shine simply because these sightless ones fail to see it; rather is this darkness due to their own inability to see.

(From Encyclical *Humani generis*, August 15, 1950)

[5] Catherine de Hueck Doherty, Servant of God

The acceptance of this truth [all that I am, all that I have is from God] will make you truly free, free to love and serve...It will also make you free to love and serve God more passionately, more constantly, more totally. You will then be on the threshold of this many-faceted, infinitely beautiful virtue and attitude of heart, state of life. That is poverty!

But still you will only have begun. I repeat, you will be only standing on the threshold of poverty's dwelling.

The next step is having a heart wide open to grace!

Now you will enter an unknown terrain through which God Himself will deign to lead you. All you have to do is to be open to grace.

(From *Dearly Beloved*, Volume 1)

[6] St. Augustine

Remember this. When people choose to withdraw far from a fire, the fire continues to give warmth, but they grow cold. When people choose to withdraw far from light, the light continues to be bright in itself but they are in darkness. This is also the case when people withdraw from God.

(From *Instructions to Novices* by Blessed Hyacinthe-Marie Cormier, O.P.)

[7] Blessed Alvaro del Portillo

It is only in prayer, in the intimacy of a face-to-face and personal dialogue with God which opens up the mind and heart (cf. Acts 16:14), that the man of faith can deepen his understanding of God's will with respect to his own life.

(From *On Priesthood*)

[8] St. Theophilus of Antioch

Man, influenced by prejudices or stirred up by his passions or bad will, is not only able to deny the evidence of external signs plain to be seen before his very eyes, but can also resist and reject the higher inspirations God infuses into his soul.

(From *Apology to Antolycus*, Book I, 2)

[9] Paul Thigpen, Ph.D

No matter who you are – whether or not you know it – you have a mortal enemy who wants to destroy you, not just in this life, but in the next. It's a spiritual war with crucial consequences in your everyday life. And the outcome of that war will determine your eternal destiny.

(From *Manual* for *Spiritual Warfare* by Dr. Paul Thigpen)

[10] St. John Paul II

Make a particular effort to seek Jesus and attain a deep personal faith which influences and directs your whole life; but above all may your commitments and plans consist in loving Jesus, with a sincere, genuine and personal love. He should be your friend and your support along the way of life. He alone has the words of eternal life.

(From January 30, 1979 Address)

[11]   St. Teresa of Calcutta

If sometimes our poor people have had to die of starvation, it is not because God didn't care for them, but because you and I didn't give, were not instruments of love in the hands of God, to give them that bread, to give them that clothing; because we did not recognize Him, when once more Christ came in distressing disguise – in the hungry man, in the lonely man, in the homeless child, seeking for shelter.

(From The Kiss of Jesus by Donna Marie Cooper O'Boyle)

[12]   St. Augustine

He who loves his neighbor must do as much good for his body as for his soul. This does not consist only in calling in the doctor, but also in caring for his neighbor's welfare – his food, his drink, his clothing, his lodging, and protecting his body from anything that might be harmful to him…They are merciful who put consideration and humanity into providing what is necessary for resisting any type of evil and alleviating pain.

(From On the Customs of the Catholic Church)

[13]   Father Jose Orlandis

A Christianity from which we tried to remove the cross of voluntary mortification and penance under the pretext that these practices are the remains of the Dark Ages or of an outworn Medieval era, quite inappropriate for a modern Humanistic Age, would be an insipid Christianity, a Christianity in name only. It would not have kept intact the doctrine of the Gospels, nor would it serve to induce men to follow in Christ's footsteps.

(From The Eight Beatitudes)

[14]   Father Benedict Baur, O.S.B.

The thought of the punishment we deserve for our sins helps us to face the daily difficulties and deprivations and struggles without which there cannot be any real freedom from sin or any perfect union with God. We always have, indeed, plenty of reason to be penetrated with the fear of God, when we consider the many occasions of sin that lie all around us, our own extreme weakness, the strength of our inordinate attachments and habits, our natural inclination to self-indulgence, the pull of our own concupiscence from within and the attractions of the world without, our many faults and defects and the plain carelessness of which we are guilty every day.

(From *Frequent Confessions*)

[15] St. Ambrose

Remove, Lord Jesus, the rottenness of my sins. While You hold me bound with bonds of love, cure what is sick within me...I have met a Physician Who lives in heaven and pours out His medicine on earth. Only He can cure my wounds, for He Himself has none; only He can remove sorrow from my heart, wanness from my soul, for He alone knows my innermost secrets.

(From *Treatise on St. Mark's Gospel*)

[16] St. John Paul II

There are incomparably more events than such visible actions whose importance to society remains hidden for the time being. There is, for example, the immense multitude of souls who have spent the whole of their existence giving themselves in the anonymity of the home, the factory, the office. There are those who have consumed themselves in anonymity amid the praying society of the cloister; those who have immolated themselves in daily martyrdom of protracted illness. The day that everything is brought out into the public gaze when the Lord comes again, everyone will see the decisive role that the humble and the inconspicuous have played, in spite of all appearances to the contrary, in the unrolling of the history of the world. And this will also be a cause of joy for the blessed, who will derive from it a theme of everlasting praise of the God who is three times Holy.

(From *February 11, 1981 Homily*)

[17] St. John of the Cross

All you who are tormented and afflicted, laboring beneath the burden of anxiety and desire, cast it aside by coming unto Me, and I will refresh you; and your souls shall find that rest of which your desires rob you.

(From *The Ascent of Mount Carmel*)

[18] St. Josemaria Escriva

...we shall not call injustice, justice; we shall not say that an offense against God is not an offense against God, or that evil is good. When confronted by evil we shall not reply with another evil, but rather with sound doctrine and good actions: drowning evil in an abundance of good (cf. Rom 12:21). That's how Christ will reign in our souls and in the souls of the people around us.

(From *Christ Is Passing Us By*)

[19] St. Francis de Sales

Bees live and feed on bitter food when making their honey; in the same way, we can never practice gentleness and patience or produce honey from such excellent virtues more surely than when eating the bread of bitterness and living in the midst of afflictions.

(From *Introduction to the Devout Life*)

[20] St. Thomas Aquinas, O.P.

The omnipotence of God is shown, above all, in the act of his forgiveness and the use of his mercy, for the way he has of showing His supreme power is to pardon freely...

(From *Summa Theologiae*, I, q25, a3, ad3)

[21] St. John Paul II

The prudent person is not, as is so often believed, the man who shrewdly knows how to make his way in the world and make the most of it for himself. He is, rather, the one who manages to construct the role of his life in accordance with the voice of a right conscience and the demands of sound morals.

We can then see that prudence is the keystone by which we each accomplish the fundamental task we have been given by God. This task is the perfection of man himself [holiness].

(From October 25, 1978 Address)

[22] Venerable Fulton J. Sheen

Our choice [...] is to be made among three dogmas: Whether man is a tool of the State, as the totalitarian believes; or whether man is an animal, as the secularist tradition of the Western World – including too many Americans – believe; or whether man is a creature made to the image and likeness of God, as the Christian believes.

(From *The Crisis In Christendom*)

[23] Father Eugene Boylan, O.C.R.

One of the reasons why men are so prone to praise one another, to overestimate their own value and abilities, to resent anything that tends to lower them in their own eyes or in the eyes of others, is that they see no hope for happiness outside themselves. That is why they are often so hyper-sensitive, so resentful when they are criticized, so upset by anyone who contradicts them, so insistent on getting their own way, so desirous of being well known, so anxious to be praised, so determined to control their surroundings. They secure themselves like a shipwrecked man holding on to a straw. And life goes on, and they move further and further away from happiness...

(From *This Tremendous Lover*)

[24] St. John Chrysostom

What do you want us to do? Go up into the mountains and become monks? What you are saying makes me want to cry. You think that modesty and chastity are just for monks? No. Christ laid down common laws for all of us. And so, when He said: 'everyone who looks at a woman lustfully' (Matthew 5:28), He was not speaking to a monk, but to the man in the street...I do not forbid you to marry, nor do I forbid you to enjoy life. I only ask that you do this with temperance, not with impurity; not with countless sins. I do not lay it down as a law that you go into the mountains and out into the deserts. I want you to be good, modest and chaste even though you are in the middle of the world.

(From *Homilies on St. Matthew's Gospel*)

[25] St. Francis de Sales

One has to suffer, in patience, the setbacks to our perfection, doing whatever we can to make progress in good spirit. We hope with patience, and instead of getting frustrated at having done so little in the past, we try diligently to do more in the future.

(From *The Art of Profiting from our Mistakes*)

[26] Father Francis Wendell, O.P.

We live in a secularist society. Stated that bluntly it means very little. Actually, the implications are tremendous. St. Dominic, were he introduced to our society, would be amazed and aghast at the things that are commonplace today. God was a reality in the lives of the people of his age; for us God had become either a myth or has been relegated to the position of a peculiar old relative who is kept more or less hidden away upstairs.

(From *Spiritual Powerhouse*)

[27] St. John Paul II

...the loss of a sense of sin is thus a form or consequence of 'the denial of God': not only in the form of atheism, but also in the form of secularism. If sin is the breaking off of one's filial relationship to God in order to situate one's life outside the obedience to Him, then to sin is not merely to deny God. To sin is also to live as if He did not exist, to eliminate Him from one's daily life.

(From Apostolic Exhortation, *Reconciliatio et Poentientia*)

[28] Father Francis Fernandez

Apostolic zeal, the desire to draw many people to Our Lord, does not require us to do anything odd or peculiar, and much less to neglect our family, social or professional duties. It is precisely in those situations – in our family, at work, with our friends, in everyday human relationships – that we find scope for an apostolic activity which may often be silent, but which is always efficacious.

(*In Conversation With God*, Volume 4:75.2)

[29] St. Catherine of Siena

We must, then, very conscientiously free our heart and affection from this tyrant, the world, and set it on God, completely free and sincere, letting nothing come between ourselves and Him. We must not be two-faced or love falsely, since He is our dear God, and He keeps His eyes on us, seeing our hidden and inmost heart.

(*Catherine of Siena: An Anthology - Volume 1*)

[30] St. Josemaria Escriva

This and no other is the end of the Church: the salvation of souls, one by one. For this the Father sent the Son. And, Jesus said, 'even so I send you' (John 20:21). From this rises the command to make His doctrine known and to baptize, so that the Most Blessed Trinity may reside in the soul, through grace.

(From *In Love With the Church*)

[31] Saint Bede

The treasure of a soul is the same as the root of a tree. A person with a treasure of patience and charity in his soul produces beautiful fruits: he loves his neighbor, and possesses other qualities that Jesus recommends; he loves his enemies, does good to those who hate him, blesses those who curse him and prays for the one who slanders him. But the man who has a source of evil in his soul does the exact opposite; he hates his friends, speaks badly of the one who loves him, and does all the other things condemned by the Lord.

(From *Commentary on St. Luke's Gospel*)

[32] Venerable Louis of Granada, O.P.

Among the works comprising charity to our neighbor the following are the most important: advice, counsel, succor, forbearance, pardon, edification. These are so strongly linked with charity that the practice of them indicates the progress we have made in the practice of this greatest of virtues.

(From *The Sinner's Guide*)

[33] St. Augustine

What better words may we carry in our heart, pronounce with our mouth, write with a pen, than the words, 'Thanks be to God'? There is no phrase that may be said so readily, that can be heard with greater joy, felt with more emotion or produced with greater effect.

(From *Letter 72*)

[34] St. John Paul II

The rich man was condemned because he did not pay attention to the other man. Because he failed to take notice of Lazarus, the person who sat at his door and who longed to eat the scraps from his table.

(From *Homily* at Yankee Stadium, October 2, 1979)

[35] Venerable Fulton J Sheen

As a man must be born before he can begin to lead his physical life, so he must be born to lead a Divine Life. That birth occurs in the Sacrament of Baptism. To survive, he must be nourished by Divine Life; that is done in the Sacrament of the Holy Eucharist.

(From Real Presence Eucharistic Education and Adoration Association)

[36] Vatican Council II

One of the gravest errors of our time is the dichotomy between the faith which many profess and the practice of their daily lives…The Christian who shirks his temporal duties shirks his duties towards his neighbor, neglects God Himself, and endangers his eternal salvation. Let Christians follow the example of Christ who worked as a craftsman; let them be proud of the opportunity to carry out their earthly activity in such a way as to integrate human, domestic, professional, scientific and ethical enterprises with religious values, under whose supreme direction all things are ordered to the glory of God.

(From *Gaudium et spes*)

[37] Blessed Pope Paul VI

The dialogue of salvation is not based on the personal merits of those with whom it is carried out or on the results that may or may not come about. Our Lord teaches: 'It is not the healthy who need a physician...'

The dialogue concerning salvation is open to everyone without distinction. Similarly, our own conversations should be potentially universal and capable of embracing all.

(From Encyclical, *Ecclesiam suam*)

[38] C.S. Lewis

Enemy-occupied territory – that is what this world is. Christianity is the story of how the rightful king has landed, you might say landed in disguise, and is calling us all to take part in a great campaign of sabotage.

(From *Mere Christianity*)

[39] Father Federico Suarez

Silence is an indispensable condition for keeping things and pondering them in one's heart. Profundity of thought can develop only in a climate of silence. Too much chatter exhausts our inner strength; it dissipates everything of any value in our heart, which becomes like a bottle of perfume left open for a long time: only water remains with a slight touch of its former fragrance.

(From *Mary of Nazareth*)

[40] St. Thomas Aquinas, O.P.

To say that someone is full of mercy is like saying his heart is full of woe. He experiences the miseries of another with the same force and sadness as if they were His own. He makes His best effort to remedy the problem because it has become His problem. This is the effect of mercy. Of course, God does not become saddened by thus making His own the miseries of His creatures. Yet He does work to remedy those problems, those defects, because to act in this way does correspond to His Divine nature.

(From *Summa Theologiae*, 1, q. 21, a.3)

[41] St. Josemaria Escriva

Be a Eucharistic soul! If the center around which your thoughts and hopes turn is the Tabernacle, then my child, how abundant the fruits of sanctity and apostolate will be!

(From *The Forge*)

[42] St. Alphonsus Liguori

Why are the prayers of Mary so highly regarded by God? Let us remember that the prayers of the saints are the prayers of His servants. But the prayers of Mary are the prayers of His Mother. This is the reason for their efficacy and authority. Since Jesus has an incredible love for His Mother, He responds to her every request...

(From *Abbreviated Sermons*, 48)

[43] St. Theophilus of Antioch

God gives sight to those who are capable of seeing Him. This is because the eyes of their mind are open to Him. Everyone has eyes, but some people keep them screened from the light of the sun. They cannot see the sun at all. But even though the blind cannot see the sun, it continues to shine. So the people who can't see ought to blame their inability to see on their own defective vision.

(*In Conversation With God*, 5:53.2)

[44] St. John Paul II

Humanity is loved by God! This very simple yet profound proclamation is owed to humanity by the Church. Each Christian's words and life must make this proclamation resound.

(From Apostolic Exhortation, *Christifedeles laici*)

[45] Marie Dominique Philippe, O.P.

It is difficult for God to manifest His Will to us without our wholehearted desire to serve Him in all things. However, the Lord acts in our life only to the extent that we allow Him to do so. He always respects our human freedom and never imposes Himself.

(From *The Mysteries of Mary*)

[46] Justice Antonin Scalia

[Christ's] message was not the need to eliminate hunger or misery or misfortune, but rather the need for each individual to love and help the hungry, the miserable, and the unfortunate. To the extent that the State takes upon itself one of the corporal works of mercy that could and would have been undertaken privately, it deprives individuals of an opportunity for sanctification and deprives the Body of Christ of an occasion for the interchange of love among its members. I wonder to what extent the decimation of women's religious orders throughout the West is attributable to the governmentalization of charity. Consider how many orphanages, hospitals, schools and homes for the elderly used to be provided by orders of nuns. They're almost all gone – as are the nuns who ran them. The State now provides or pays for these services through salaried social workers. Even purely individual charity must surely have been affected. 'What need for me to give a beggar a handout? Do I not pay taxes for government food stamps and municipally run shelters and soup kitchens? The man asking me for a dollar probably wants it for liquor!' There is, of course, neither love nor merit in the taxes I pay for those services. I pay them because I have to…The transformation of charity into legal entitlement has produced donors without love and recipients without gratitude.

(Excerpted from *How I Got Schooled by Scrooge and Antonin Scalia*)

[47] St. Vincent of Lerins

...if one yields ground on any single point of Catholic doctrine, one will later have to yield to another, and again in another, and so on until such surrenders come to be something normal and acceptable. And, when one gets used to rejecting dogma bit by bit, the final result will be the repudiation of it altogether.

(From *Narrations*, 23)

[48] St. John Paul II

Open the gates wide to Christ! Have confidence in Him. Take the risk of following Him. Obviously, this demands that you should come out of yourselves, or your own way of reasoning, or your prudence. It demands that you leave behind your indifference, your self-sufficiency, those un-Christian habits that you have perhaps acquired. Yes, that demands renunciation, a conversion, which first of all you must want to want; want to pray for in your prayer, and want to put into practice. Let Christ be for you the way, the truth and the life. Let Him be your salvation and your happiness. Let Him take over the whole of your life so that with Him you can live it in all its dimensions. Let all your relationships, activities, feelings, thoughts, be integrated in Him, or, so to speak, 'Christified'. I wish that with Christ you may come to recognize God as the beginning and end of your existence.

(June 1, 1980, Parc des Princes)

[49] St. Alphonsus Liguori

There will be those who say: 'that is exactly why I don't go to Communion more often, because I realize my love is cold...' If you are cold, do you think it sensible to move away from the fire? Precisely because you feel your heart frozen you should go 'more frequently' to Holy Communion, provided you feel a sincere desire to love Jesus Christ. 'Go to Holy Communion', says St. Bonaventure, 'even when you feel lukewarm, leaving everything in God's hands. The more my sickness debilitates me, the more urgently do I need a doctor.

(From *The Practice of Love for Jesus*)

[50] St. John Chrysostom

Is it not ridiculous to be so meticulous about bodily things when the feast draws near, as to get out and prepare your best clothes a day ahead...and to deck yourself in your very finest, all the while paying not the slightest attention to your soul, which is abandoned, besmirched, squalid and utterly consumed by desire...?

(From *Homily 6*)

[51] Blessed John Henry Newman

Seek His Face Who ever dwells in real and bodily presence in His Church. Do at least as much as the disciples did. They had but little faith; they feared; they had no great confidence or peace, but at least they did not keep away from Christ...Do not keep from Him, but, when you are in trouble, come to Him day by day, asking Him earnest and perseveringly for those favors which He alone can give...So, though He discerns much infirmity in you which ought not to be there, yet He will deign to rebuke the winds and the sea, and say: 'Peace, be still.' And there will be great calm.

(From *Sermon for the Fourth Sunday after the Epiphany*)

[52] St. Thomas Aquinas, O.P.

God prepares whomsoever He desires for a specific mission. He also grants the particular person the necessary graces to carry out that task they are entrusted with.

(From *Summa Theologiae, 2, q27, a4*)

[53] St. Bernard

O Jesus..., how consoling You are to those who invoke You! How good You are to those who seek You! What will You not be to those who find

You! Only he who has felt it can know what it is to languish in love for thee, O Jesus!

(In Conversation With God, 1:40.2)

[54] St. John Paul II

Those confessionals scattered about the world where men declare their sins don't speak of the severity of God. Rather do they speak of His mercy. And all those who approach the confessional, sometimes after many years weighed down with mortal sins, in the moment of getting rid of this intolerable burden, find at last a longed-for relief. They find joy and tranquility of conscience which, outside Confession, they will never be able to find anywhere.

(From March 16, 1980 Homily)

[55] St. Augustine

For there was a hunger within me from a lack of that inner food, which is Yourself, my God. Yet by that hunger I did not hunger, but was without desire for incorruptible food, not because I was already filled with it, but because the more empty I was, the more distaste I had for it.

(From Confessions)

[56] Father Federico Suarez

If there are so many Christians who today live aimlessly with little depth, and hemmed in on all sides by narrow horizons, it is due, above all, to their lack of any clear idea of why they, personally exist...What elevates a man and truly gives him a personality of his own is the consciousness of his vocation, the consciousness of his own specific task in the universe.

(From Mary of Nazareth)

[57] Father Francis Fernandez

During the three years of His public life, He [Jesus] has healed many people, he has freed those possessed by the devil, He has raised the dead...But He did not heal all the sick people in the world, nor did He eliminate all the sufferings of this life, *for pain is not an absolute evil*, as sin is, and it can have an incomparable redemptive value, if we unite it to the suffering of Christ.

(From *In Conversations With God*, 3:13.1)

[58] St. Alphonsus Liguori

And what are we to do in the presence of the Blessed Sacrament? Love Him. Praise Him. Thank Him. Ask of Him. What does a poor man do in the presence of a wealthy man? What does a sick person do in the presence of a doctor? What does a thirsty person do at the sight of a fountain of sparkling water?

(From *Visits to the Blessed Sacrament*)

[59] St. John Paul II

...we must pray because we are fragile and culpable. We need to admit humbly and truly that we are poor creatures, with confused ideas...We are fragile and weak, and in constant need of interior strength and consolation. Prayer gives us strength for great ideals, for keeping our faith, charity, purity, generosity; prayer gives us strength to rise up from indifference and guilt, if we have had the misfortune to give in to temptation and weakness. Prayer gives us light by which to see and to judge from God's perspective and from eternity. That is why you must not give up praying! Don't let a day go by without praying a little! Prayer is a duty, but is also a joy because it is a dialogue with God through Jesus Christ!

(From March 14, 1979 Audience)

[60] Francis Joseph Sheed

I cannot say how often I have been told that some old Irishman saying his rosary is holier than I am with all my study. I daresay he is. For his own sake, I hope he is. But if the only evidence is that he knows less theology than I, then it is evidence that would convince neither him nor me. It would not convince him, because all those rosary-loving, tabernacle-loving old Irishmen I have ever known (and my own ancestry is rich with them) were avid for more knowledge of the Faith. It does not convince me because while it is obvious that an ignorant man can be virtuous, it is equally obvious that ignorance is not a virtue; men have been martyred who could not have stated a doctrine of the Church correctly, and martyrdom is the supreme proof of love: yet with more knowledge of God they would have loved Him still more.

(From *Theology for Beginners*)

[61] C. Lopez Pardo

Life is passing. We are constantly coming across people from the most varied walks of life. What a lot remains to be done...How many words still have to be spoken...Certainly we have to start by doing (cf. Acts 1:1); but then, too, we have to speak; each ear, each heart, each mind has its own moment, its friendly voice that can call it out of its slough of despondency, and encourage it to rise out of its present state of unhappiness.

If we love God, we cannot fail to feel the reproach of the days that pass, of the people (often so close to us) who pass by, ungreeted, unhailed...without our being able to do whatever it was that was needed, without our even knowing how to say what we should have said.

(From *On Life and Death*)

[62] Jean-Baptiste Chautard, O.C.S.O.

Preaching by example will always be the foremost instrument of conversion...Lectures, good books, Christian newspapers and magazines, and even fine sermons must gravitate around this fundamental program: that we need to influence people by an apostolate of good example, the example of fervent Christians, who make Jesus Christ live again on this earth by spreading about them the good odor of His virtues."

(From *The Soul of the Apostolate*)

[63] Reginald Garrigou-Lagrange, O.P.

In those persons who we are not naturally attracted to, we have to see souls that have been saved by the Blood of Christ, souls that belong to the Mystical Body of Christ, souls which might even be closer to His Sacred Heart than our own. It often happens that we spend many years alongside very beautiful souls without our ever noticing it.

(From *The Three Conversions of the Interior Life*)

[64] St. Augustine

Every age is an age of martyrdom. Don't say that Christians are not suffering persecution; the Apostles words are always true...All who desire to live a godly life in Christ Jesus will be persecuted (2 Tim 3:12). All, with no one being excluded or exempted. If you want to test the truth of this saying, you have only to begin to lead a pious life and you will see what good reason he had for saying this.

(From *Sermon 6*)

[65] Caryll Houselander

You see, *God's* will for you is to serve Him, in His way, as He chooses, *now*. It is only a want of humility to think of extreme vocations, like being a nun or a nurse, while you try to bypass your present obvious vocation, which is to restore your will to God's, so that you may become what *He* wants you to be, and may be able to use the faculties He has given to you for His service.

(From *The Letters of Caryll Houselander: Her Spiritual Legacy*)

[66] Blessed Pope Paul VI

The preacher of the Gospel will therefore be a person who, even at the price of personal renunciation and suffering, always seeks the truth that he must transmit to others. He never betrays or hides truth out of a desire to please men, in order to astonish or shock, nor for the sake of originality or a desire to make an impression.

(From Apostolic Exhortation, *Evangeli nuntiandi*, December 8, 1975)

[67] St. Mechtildis

Oh, if men did but know how much they might increase their glory and their merit every day, they would never awaken in the morning without gratitude in their hearts to God for His goodness in giving them another day in which they might increase their glory in heaven, their eternal home.

(From *The Way To God*)

[68] St. Jerome

With a Christian, not the beginning but the end is what is important. St. Paul had a bad beginning but a good end. Judas had a good beginning but a bad end.

(From *Illustrations From Sermons and Instructions*)

[69] St. Francis de Sales

Holy Mass is the sum of all spiritual exercises, the mainspring of devotion, the soul of piety, the fire of divine charity, the abyss of divine mercy, and a precious means whereby God confers on us His graces.

(From *Introduction to the Devout Life*)

[70] St. Josemaria Escriva

We children of God have to be contemplatives; people, who, in the midst of the din of the throng, know how to find silence of soul in a lasting conversation with Our Lord, people who know how to look at Him as they look at a Father, as they look at a Friend, as they look at someone with whom they are madly in love.

(From *The Forge*)

[71] St. Leo the Great

Whoever truly wishes to venerate the Passion of the Lord should contemplate Jesus crucified with eyes of his soul, and in such a way that he identifies his own body with that of Jesus.

(From *Sermon 15 on the Passion*)

[72] St. Alphonsus Liguori

But God is merciful. Behold another common delusion by which the devil encourages sinners to persevere in sin! A certain author has said that more souls have been sent to hell by the mercy of God than by His justice. This indeed is the case; for men are induced by the deceits of the devil to persevere in sin, through confidence in God's mercy; and thus, they are lost.

(From *The Sermons of St. Alphonsus Liguori: For All the Sundays of the Year*)

[73] Madeleine Delbrel, Servant of God

In the area of God's work, we are all assigned precise tasks, for it is God who initiated each work and brings each to completion. He works unceasingly; He doesn't give us the leisure to mess around doing nothing.

(From *The Joy of Believing*)

[74] Brother Lawrence of the Resurrection

It is not necessary for being with God to always be at church. We make an oratory of our heart wherein to retire from time to time to converse with Him in meekness, humility, and love. Everyone is capable of such familiar conversation with God, some more, some less. He knows what we can do. Let us begin then.

(From *The Practice of the Presence of God*)

[75] St. Teresa of Avila

I would accept Purgatory until the Last Judgment to deliver but one of them [souls]. And what do I care how long I suffer, if I can thus set free a single soul, let alone many souls, for the greater glory of God.

(From *The Interior Castle*)

[76] Juan Donoso Cortes

Those who pray do more for the world than those who fight, and if the world is going from bad to worse, it is because there are more battles than prayers.

(From *The Soul of the Apostolate*)

[77] St. Augustine

In former times, Christians were incited to renounce Christ; now they are taught to deny Christ. Then they were forced, now they are taught; then violence was used, now it is deception; then one heard the shouts of the enemy; now, when he prowls around, gentle and insinuating, it is difficult to recognize him. Everyone knows how he tried to force Christians to deny Christ; he tried to attract them to himself so that they would renounce him; but they confessed Christ and were crowned by Him. Now they are taught to deny Christ by trickery, because he doesn't want them to realize that he is drawing them away from Christ.

(From *Commentaries on the Psalms*, 39:1)

[78] Blessed Henry Suso, O.P.

[Jesus speaking] Sometimes a clear eye is as quickly blinded by flour as by gray ashes. Could the presence of any human being be more harmless than My presence among my beloved disciples? There were no unnecessary words, no unrestrained gestures, no conversations which began with spiritual topics, and end in useless babbling. True earnestness and complete, absolute truth dominated all our intercourse. Yet, my bodily presence had to be withdrawn in order to prepare the disciples to receive the Spirit. How great an obstacle, therefore, can human presence be. Before men are led into themselves by one person, they are drawn outward by thousands; before they are once taught with doctrine, they are many times confused by bad example.

(From *Little Book of Eternal Wisdom*)

[79] St. Josemaria Escriva

...prayer is not a question of what you say or feel, but of Love. And you love when you try to say something to the Lord, even though you might not actually say anything.

(From *Furrow*)

[80] Vatican II

Christ the Lord founded one Church and one Church only. However, many communions present themselves to men as the true inheritors of Jesus Christ; all indeed profess to be the followers of the Lord, but they differ in mind and go their different ways, as if Christ Himself is divided. Certainly, such division openly contradicts the Will of Christ, scandalizes the world, and damages the most holy cause, the preaching of the Gospel to every creature.

(From *Decree on Ecumenism*)

[81] St. John Paul II

...the presence of the devil in the history of humanity is increased in the measure that man and society are separated from God.

(General Audience - August 20, 1986)

[82] Catherine de Hueck Doherty, Servant of God

One has to begin at the beginning. The beginning is to finally acknowledge *your own immense poverty*. Now you have to fully, deeply realize that *all that you are, all that you have is from God!* From this follows that you have and are *nothing*.

Once you make this truth of your own poverty before God the very marrow of your thoughts, your life, your love, your body, in a word, your very being, then you will become truly humble. Then you will walk in truth, walk in and with God...

(From How Poor Can You Get? by Father David May)

[83] Father Federico Suarez

If there are so many Christians who today live aimlessly with little depth, and hemmed in on all sides by narrow horizons, it is due, above all, to their lack of any clear idea of why they, personally exist...What elevates a man and truly gives him a personality of his own is the consciousness of his vocation, the consciousness of his own specific task in the universe.

(From Mary of Nazareth)

[84] St. Alphonsus Liguori

The good morals and the salvation of the people depend on good pastors. If there is a good priest in charge of a parish, you will soon see devotion flourishing, people frequenting the sacraments and honoring the practice of mental prayer. Hence the proverb: like pastor, like parish.

(From The Soul of the Apostolate)

[85] Father Francis Fernandez

The real place of the laity is not the sacristy, but the family, business, fashion and sport…fields of endeavor in which in their own right they must try to bring God. The mission of the laity must lead them to imbue family, work and the social order with the Christian principles that raise these areas of human living to the supernatural order and thus make them more human; the laity's business is the dignity and primacy of the human person, social solidarity, the sanctity of marriage, responsible freedom, love for the truth, respect for justice on all levels, the spirit of service, and the practice of mutual understanding and of charity…

(From *In Conversation With God*, Vol 7:10.2)

[86] Cardinal Pietro Parolin

In the midst of great concern and uncertainty about the future, what does Fatima ask of us? Perseverance in the consecration to the Immaculate Heart of Mary, shown by the daily recitation of the Rosary. And what if, despite our prayers, wars continue? Even though immediate results may not be evident, let us persevere in prayer. Prayer is never useless. Sooner or later, it will bear fruit…Prayer is capital in the hands of God: He turns it to good account in His own times and ways, which are very different from our own.

(From Homily at Fatima - May 12, 2017 Vigil Mass)

[87] Whittaker Chambers

…life and faith must be *one*. That is, the individual must not only have a lively faith, but must *live his faith*. He must believe with his whole being what he professes with his lips. He must say aloud his *Credo*, not with words, but with every action of his life. He must be a Catholic not only for the hour or so he spends in church on Sunday, but he must *be* Christ twenty-four hours a day, seven days a week, fifty-two weeks of the year.

(From *God, A Woman and the Way*)

[88] St. Augustine

Don't go astray in the mist and the fog, but rather listen to the voice of the shepherd. Fall back on holy Scripture, there you will find the delight of your heart; you will find nothing there that will harm or poison you; rich is the food you will find there.

(From *Sermon 46 on Shepherds*)

[89] St. Bernard of Clairvaux

You were afraid to approach the Father...so He gave you Jesus as your mediator. Mary has given Him to you as your Brother. But, perhaps, you fear even Jesus; for in Him there is Divine Majesty since, although He became Man, He, nevertheless, remained God. Do you wish to have an Advocate with Him? Turn to Mary...The Son will hear His Mother; and the Father will hear the Son. My little children, this is the ladder for sinners. This is my greatest confidence. This, the whole reason for my hope.

(From *The Great Means of Salvation and of Perfection*)

[90] Pope Pius XI

Christ must reign in our *minds* – which must assent firmly and submissively to all revealed truth and to Christ's teachings. He must reign in our *wills* – which should bow in obedience to God's laws and precepts. He must reign in our *hearts* – which, turning aside from all natural desires, should love God above all things and cling to Him alone. He should reign in our *bodies* and *members*, which should serve as instruments of our soul's sanctification.

(From Encyclical *Quas Primas*)

[91] Rev. M. Raymond, O.C.S.O.

This morning, I, and every priest who offered the Holy Sacrifice, took an almost weightless wafer of wheat, a drop of water, and a very insignificant amount of wine – three very ordinary, and truly insignificant things, no matter how we view them – and we offered them to God. Certainly, in a world such as ours, these three things, plus a few words my fellow priests and I spoke, amount to nothing. Yet, when touched by God, when taken by Christ, when transubstantiated, what in the world can compare with them?

Of the three things offered, neither you nor I, by ordinary vision, could see anything of the water; and of the wheat and the wine, the appearances remained just as insignificant after Consecration as before. But how deceiving are those appearances!

The dynamism and power said to be latent in certain atoms, is as nothing compared to the Power in what looks like a tiny wafer of wheat and a half ounce of wine. Omnipotence is there. And so with our significant lives and the truly insignificant acts that fill them. Once they are placed in Christ Jesus, touched by God, taken into His Christ, they can save the world.

(From *God, A Woman and The Way*)

[92] Catherine de Hueck Doherty, Servant of God

The naked crucified One always knows His own, and [He] especially cannot resist the ones who strip themselves inwardly naked for Him and immolate themselves with Him on His own cross for love of Him and for the souls for whom He dies.

Stripped in this fashion, dying to self, crucified through poverty and obedience, walking in humility which is truth, you will be able to feel what the poor feel. You will heal, console, and bring multitudes to God. You will be truly poor in the full sense of that glorious word, and hence truly rich.

(From *Dearly Beloved, Volume 1*)

[93] Brother Lawrence of the Resurrection

I know that for the right practice of it [the presence of God] the heart must be empty of all other things, because God will possess the heart alone; and as He cannot possess it alone without emptying it of all besides, so neither can He act there, and do in it what He pleases, unless it be left vacant for Him.

(From *The Practice of the Presence of God*)

[94] Father Charles Arminjon

Remove the fear of eternal punishment from mankind, and the world will be filled with crime...Hell will simply happen sooner; instead of being postponed until the future life, it will be inaugurated in the midst of humanity, in the present life.

(From *The End of the Present World*)

[95] St. Maximilian Kolbe

[The apostolate] is a collaboration (if such is the correct word) with God Himself in the work of perfection, of sanctification...In view of this work, therefore, the Savior Himself expressly commanded His apostles: 'Remain in Me and I in you' (Jn. 15:4-6)...The fruitfulness of the work, then, does not depend on ability, on energy, on money, although these, too, are gifts of God useful in the Catholic apostolate, but solely and exclusively depends on the degree of one's union with God. Should this decrease, or if such be weakened, the other means will avail nothing...eloquent sermons and works divorced from prayer bear no fruit.

(From *For the Life of the World - St Maximilian and the Eucharist*)

[96] Father Jacques Phillipe

If people know what they must do today and commit themselves to doing it and leave tomorrow to God's providence, all is well. What more can anyone do? Take the step that needs taking today. Take another step tomorrow. Every day will have its own steps to take.

(From March 20, 2017 Reflections of the Frassati Fellowship - New York City)

[97] Rev. M. Raymond, O.C.S.O.

To human eyes how did Jesus differ from the thieves who were condemned and crucified with Him? If some stranger had come to Jerusalem that Friday afternoon and passed Calvary before darkness enfolded it, how could he tell that the middle cross held Innocence and the Redemption of mankind? He would have seen three naked men dying by degrees. How could he know that One was not only the Light of the World but the Life of all living? Mary had eyes of flesh and she saw the beaten, bloody body of her Son upon the nails. She saw that body taken down. She held it. She counted the wounds. She untangled the blood-matted hair. She folded the nerveless arms. She closed the gaping mouth. She straightened the lifeless legs. She knew she was holding a corpse. Yet in that corpse she adored the Christ of God and the Jesus of men. Was there ever such faith on earth?

(From *God, A Woman and the Way*)

[98] St. Pius X

Without interior life, we will never have the strength to persevere in sustaining all the difficulties inseparable from any apostolate, the coldness and lack of co-operation even on the part of virtuous men, the calumnies of our adversaries, and at times even the jealousy of friends and comrades in arms…Only a patient virtue, unshakably based upon the good, and at the same time smooth and tactful, is able to move these difficulties to one side and diminish their power.

(From June 11, 1905 Encyclical to the Priests of Italy)

[99] St. Augustine

There is no sin or crime committed by another which I myself am not capable of committing through my weakness; and if I have not committed it, it is because God, in his mercy, has not allowed me to and has preserved me in the good.

(From *Confessions*)

[100] Blessed Alvaro del Porillo

[What do people want and expect from the priest:] They need, desire and hope – perhaps without thus consciously reasoning out such a need or hope – for a priest who is a priest one hundred percent; a man who shows an ardent concern for them by opening up new horizons for their souls, who exercises his ministry without ceasing, and who has a big heart capable of understanding and loving everyone, though at times his concern may not be reciprocated.

(From *On The Priesthood*)

Pondering Tidbits of Truth – Volume 4

Individuals Quoted

(Page references are within parenthesis)

Alvaro del Portillo (Blessed) (1914–1994) Spanish priest and Bishop who succeeded St. Josemaria Escriva as the prelate of *Opus Dei* (3 and 31)

Ambrose (Saint) (340-397) Bishop of Milan and Doctor of the Church (5)

Thomas Aquinas (O.P.) (Saint) (1225-1274) Italian Dominican priest, philosopher, theologian, Doctor of the Church (6, 12 and 16)

Charles Armijon (Father) 19th century French priest and author of *End of the Present World* (29)

Augustine (Saint) (354-430) Bishop of Hippo, philosopher, theologian and writer (1, 2, 4, 10, 17, 20, 23, 27 and 31)

Bede (Saint) (672-735) English monk, devoted to the study of Scripture and to writing and teaching (10)

Benedict Baur (O.S.B.) (Father) (1877-1963) Benedictine priest and spiritual writer (4)

Bernard of Clairvaux (Saint) (1091-1153) French Abbot, reformer of Cistercian Order, and spiritual writer (16 and 27)

Eugene Boylan (O.C.R.) (Father) (1904-1963) Irish born Trappist monk and writer (7)

Catherine of Siena (Saint) (1347-1380) Lay tertiary of the Dominican Order, mystic, Doctor of the Church, one of the two patron saints of Italy (9)

Whittaker Chambers (1901-1961) American editor and journalist, former Communist spy and leader of Conservative movement in U.S.(26)

Jean-Baptiste Chautard, O.C.S.O. (1858-1935) Trappist Abbot and author, whose book *The Soul of The Apostolate*, was valued by St. Pius X and Pope Benedict XV (19)

John Chrysostom (Saint) (344-407) Eloquent preacher, theologian, liturgist, Archbishop of Constantinople, and a Doctor of the Church (8 and 16)

John of the Cross (Saint) (1542-1591) Spanish mystic and priest who, along with St. Teresa of Avila, founded the Discalced Carmelites (6)

Juan Donoso Cortes (1809-1853) Spanish diplomat, author and political theorist (23)

Madeleine Delbrel (Servant of God) (1904-1964) French Catholic author, poet and mystic (22)

Catherine de Hueck Doherty (Servant of God) (1896-1985) Wife, mother, social activist, author and founder of Madonna House Apostolate, a Catholic community of lay men, women and priests (2, 25 and 28)

Josemaria Escriva (Saint) (1902-1975) Spanish priest, author and founder of *Opus Dei* (1, 6, 9, 13, 21 and *24)*

Francis de Sales (Saint) (1567-1622) Bishop of Geneva, preacher and spiritual writer (6, 8 and 21)

Francis Fernandez (Father) Spanish priest, author and member of *Opus Dei* born in 1938 (9, 17 and 26)

Reginald Garrigou-Lagrange, O.P. (1877-1964) French Dominican priest, author, theologian, and lecturer; considered one of the greatest Catholic theologians of the 20th century (20)

Caryll Houselander (1901-1954) Catholic artist, mystic, religious writer and poet (20)

Jerome (Saint) (347-420) priest, apologist, Doctor of the Church, best known for his translation of the Bible into Latin (21)

Maximilian Kolbe (Saint) (1894-1941) Polish Conventual Franciscan friar, martyr, and known as the Apostle of Consecration to Mary (29)

Jean-Baptiste Henri Lacordaire (O.P) (1802-1861) French Dominican priest, renown preacher, theologian and journalist who helped reestablish the Dominican Order in post-Revolutionary France (1)

Lawrence of the Resurrection (1614-1691) lay brother in a Carmelite monastery in Paris (22 and 29)

Leo the Great (Saint) (Pope) (400-461) Doctor of the Church, asserted the universal jurisdiction of the Roman bishop, known as the doctrine of Petrine supremacy, and first Pope called "The Great". (22)

C.S. Lewis (1898-1963) Irish born British novelist, essayist, lay theologian and Christian apologist (12)

Louis of Granada (O.P.) (Venerable) (1505-1588) Dominican theologian, preacher and writer (10)

Alphonsus Liguori (Saint) (1698-1787) Italian Bishop, spiritual writer, theologian and founder of the Redemptorists (13, 15, 18, 22 and 25)

Mechtildis (Saint) (1125 -1160) German Benedictine nun, abbess and mystic (21)

John Henry Newman (Cardinal) (Blessed) (1801-1890) author, poet and Anglican convert to Catholicism (16)

Jose Orlandis (Father) (1918-2010) Spanish priest, Professor, spiritual writer and member of *Opus Dei* (4)

Pietro Parolin (Cardinal) (1955-) Italian Cardinal, Vatican diplomat and Secretary of State (26)

John Paul II (Saint) (Pope) (1920-2005) Pope from 1978-2005, second longest pontificate (3, 5, 7, 9, 11, 13, 15, 17, 18 and 25)

Paul VI (Pope) (Blessed) (1897-1978) reigned as Pope from June 21, 1963 through August 6, 1978. Issued the Encyclical *Humanae Vitae* (11 and 20)

Jacque Phillipe (Father) (1947-) French priest, author, retreat master, spiritual director and member of the Community of the Beatitudes (30)

Marie-Dominique Phillipe (O.P.) (Father) (1912-2006) French Dominican professor, theologian and philosopher (14)

Pius XI (Pope) (1857-1939) Served from 1922 until his death in 1939. His pontificate noted for diplomatic activity and his opposition to programs of Facist regimes. (27)

Pius XII (Pope) (Venerable) (1876-1958) Pope from March 2, 1939 to October 9, 1958 (2)

M. Raymond (O.S.C.O) (Father) Trappist priest and spiritual writer. Born in 1903 and now deceased (28 and 30)

Antonin Scalia (1936-2016) Associate Justice of the Supreme Court of the United States from 1986 until his death (14)

Francis Sheed (1897-1982) Lawyer, Catholic speaker, publisher, writer and member of the Catholic Evidence Guild (18)

Fulton Sheen (Venerable) (1895-1979) Archbishop, renowned theologian, prolific writer and best-known television and radio evangelist of his time (7 and 11)

Federico Suarez (Father) (1917-) Spanish priest, author, professor and member of *Opus Dei* (12, 17 and 25)

Henry Suso (O.P.) (Blessed) (1300-1366) Dominican priest, German mystic and author (24)

Teresa of Avila (Saint) (1511-1582) Reformer of the Carmelite Order, Doctor of the Church, spiritual writer (23)

Teresa of Calcutta (Saint) (1910-1997) Founder of the Missionary Sisters of Charity. Recipient of Nobel Peace Prize (4)

Theophilus of Antioch (Saint) (120-190) convert to Catholicism, apologist and writer (3 and 13)

Paul Thigpen (Ph.D.) Contemporary Catholic author, journalist, theology professor and current editor of TAN Books (3)

Vincent of Lerins (Saint) (died in 445) French monk and author (15)

Francis Wendell (O.P.) (Father) (Deceased) Dominican priest, author and promoter of the Lay Dominican vocation (8)

Suggested Reading

This is a listing of books and articles referenced herein which you may wish to read in their entirety:

Arminjon, Charles (Father). *The End of the Present World and the Mysteries of the Future Life*. Trans. by Susan Conroy and Peter McEnerny. Manchester, NH: Sophia Press Institute. 2008

Augustine (Saint). *Confessions of St. Augustine*. New York, NY: Doubleday. 1960

Boylan, Eugene (O.C.R.) (Father) *This Tremendous Lover*. Westminster, MD: The Newmann Press Shop. 1947

Chautard, Jean-Baptiste (O.C.S.O.). *The Soul of the Apostolate*. Charlotte, NC: TAN Books. 1946

Cooper-O'Boyle, Donna Marie. *The Kiss of Jesus*. San Francisco, CA: Ignatius Press. 2015

Cormier, Hyacinthe-Marie (O.P.) (Blessed) *Instructions For Novices*. Translators: George G. Christian, O.P. and Richard L. Christian. 2012

Domanski, Jerzy (OFM.Con.) (Father) *For The Life of the World: St. Maximilian and the Eucharist*. New Bedford, MA: Franciscans of the Immaculate. 1993

Delbrel, Madeleine (Servant of God) *The Joy of Blessing*. Montreal, Canada: Mediaspaul. 1993

DeSales, Francis (Saint) *Introduction to the Devout Life*. New York, NY: Image Books. 1950

Doherty de Heuck, Catherine (Servant of God). *Dearly Beloved, Volume 1*. Combermere, Ontario Canada: Madonna House Publications. 1989

Dorcy, Mary Jean (O.P.) (Sister) *St. Dominic's Family*. Rockford, IL: TAN Books and Publishers, Inc. 1983

Escriva, Josemaria (Saint) *In Love With His Church*. London/New York: Scepter Publishers. 2007

Escriva, Josemaria (Saint) *The Forge*. London/New York: Scepter Publishers. 1987

Escriva, Josemaria (Saint) *The Furrow*. London/New York: Scepter Publishers. 1986

Escriva, Josemaria (Saint) *The Way of the Cross*. London/New York: Scepter Publishers. 1981

Garrigou-Lagrange, Reginald (O.P.) (Father) *The Three Conversions of the Interior Life*. Rockford, IL: TAN Books sand Publishers, Inc. 1977

John of the Cross (Saint) *The Ascent of Mount Camel*. Translator: E. Allison Peers. Mineola, NY: Dover Publications. 2008

Lawrence of the Resurrection). *The Practice of the Presence of God*. New Kensington, PA: Whitaker House. 1982

Lewis, C.S. *Mere Christianity*. New York, NY: Harper Collins Publishers: 1952

Liguori, Alphonsus. (Saint) *The Great Means of Salvation and Perfection*. Kassock Bros. Publishing. 2014

Liguori, Alphonsus. (Saint) *The Practice of the Love of Jesus Christ*. Potosi, WI: St. Athanasius Press

Liguori, Alphonsus. (Saint) *The Sermons of St. Alphonsus: For All The Sundays of the Year*. Charlotte, NC: TAN Publishers. 2013

Liguori, Alphonsus. (Saint) *Visits to the Blessed Sacrament*. Rockford, IL: TAN Books and Publishers, Inc. 2001

Louis of Granada (O.P.) (Venerable) *The Sinner's Guide*. London, England: Aeterna Press. 2015

Noffke, Suzanne, (O.P.) Translator. *Catherine of Siena Anthology, Volume 1* Tempe, AZ: Medieval and Renaissance Texts and Studies, Arizona State University. 2011

Phillipe, Marie Dominique (O.P.) (Father) *The Mysteries of Mary*. Charlotte, NC: St. Benedict Press. 2011

Raymond, M. (O.C.S.O.) (Father). *God, A Woman and The Way*. Milwaukee, WI: Bruce Publishing Co. 1954

Sheed, Francis Joseph. *Theology for Beginners*. Brooklyn, NY: Angelico Press. 2013

Sheen, Fulton, J. (Venerable). *Crisis in Christendom: The Christian Order*. January 31, 1943 broadcast on *The Catholic Hour*

Suarez, Federico (Father). *Mary of Nazareth*. London, UK: Scepter Publishers. 1979

Suso, Henry O.P) (Blessed). *The Little Book of Eternal Wisdom*. Benediction Classics. 2009

Teresa of Avila (Saint.) *The Interior Castle*. Radford, VA: Wilder Publications, LLC. 2008

Thigpen, Paul Ph.D. *Manual For Spiritual Warfare*. Charlotte, NC: TAN Books. 2014

Ward, Maisie. *The Letters of Caryll Houselander: Her Spiritual Legacy*. New York, NY: Sheed and Ward. 1965

Wendell, Francis O.P. (Father) *Spiritual Powerhouse*. Washington, D.C. Dominican Publications. 1952

About the Author

Michael Seagriff practiced law for 30 years, as a general practitioner, prosecutor, criminal defense attorney and Administrative Law Judge.

His vocation as a Lay Dominican created an insatiable desire to learn, study, live and share his Faith. For more than ten years he led a Prison Ministry program and has spent more then fifteen years promoting Perpetual Eucharistic Adoration, serving as coordinator of that devotion in his former parish. He always wanted to write and share these experiences but never seemed to have the time when he was working. All that changed unexpectedly in 2009 when he retired.

Articles that he has written since retiring have been published in *Homiletic & Pastoral Review*, *The Catholic Sun*, a weekly diocesan newspaper, and on *Catholic Exchange.com CatholicLane.com, Catholic Online.com, Catholic Writers Guild Blog,* and *Zenit.org*.

The author acquired his healthy sense of humor and his love for the Catholic Faith from his deceased Dad and Mom and employs both frequently, sometimes to the joy and at other times to the consternation of those closest to him.

He blogs at: http://harvestingthefruitsofcontemplation.blogspot.com/ and at http://forgotttentruthstosetfaithafire.blogspot.com/ and at mseagrif@wordpress.com

Other Books By Author

[The **Catholic Writer's Guild** awarded its Seal of Approval to *Forgotten Truths to Set Faith Afire! Words to Challenge, Inspire and Instruct* **and** to *I Thirst For Your Love*.]

Forgotten Truths to Set Faith Afire! Words to Challenge, Inspire and Instruct

This is a compilation of over 1200 essential but Forgotten Truths that opened the author's eyes, spoke to his heart and stirred his soul. The power of these words changed his life and can do the same for all who read and reflect upon them.

*****

I Thirst For Your Love

Our Lord thirsts for our love. He is waiting for us to love Him! Why have so many of us been unwilling to quench His thirst? If we really believed Jesus Christ was truly here with us, we would visit Him. Nothing would prevent us from doing so. We would not permit anyone or anything to take precedence over Him. But we do not come as we ought because not enough of us believe He is here!

It is the author's hope that after reading *I Thirst For Your Love*, you will quench His thirst, and Love! Reverence! and Visit Him!

*****

Stirring Slumbering Souls – 250 Eucharistic Reflections

We do not treat, reverence and love our Eucharistic Lord as we ought. How many of us love Him enough to gift Him with our presence for one of the 168 hours He gives each week?

The 250 quotations in this book are intended to increase our belief in, reverence for, devotion to and love of His Eucharistic Presence, to touch lukewarm hearts, to stir slumbering souls and to re-ignite the flame of love for our loving Lord that He placed in our hearts the second He breathed life into them.

*****

Fleeting Glimpses of The Silly, Sentimental and Sublime

This book is a mini-memoir containing 20 of the author's personal memories and reflections that he hopes will bring you laughter at a time you feel forlorn, comfort when you are overburdened with the challenges of daily living, tears of joy when certain words you read or images they generate resurrect thoughts of those you loved and lost, greater appreciation for the gift of life, zeal for the salvation of your soul, and an increased desire to give to God and those He created what He and they deserve.

*****

Pondering Tidbits of Truth (Volume 1) (Volume 2) and (Volume 3)

These books recognize two realities of contemporary life: we are all busy people and many of us have convinced ourselves that we simply do not have the time to read, ponder and reflect on the wealth of spiritual wisdom our Catholic Church has accumulated over the centuries. Yet, we owe God and ourselves this reflective time.

If we spend little or no time pondering the truths and mysteries of our Faith, we are not going to progress spiritually – a growth essential to our eternal well-being and that of those around us.

Among the 100 quotations in each of these books, some may be familiar to you – others maybe not so much. All of them offer much fruit for your reflection and contemplation.

All of the author's books are available at Amazon.com.

Made in the USA
Columbia, SC
14 December 2017